Contents

KV-638-059

The Alsatian
(The German Shepherd Dog)

Joyce Ixer

John Bartholomew & Son Limited
Edinburgh and London

Dedication
*To Lulu, the grey sable who, almost fifty years ago, introduced
me to the breed to which I have been faithful ever since.*

*The Publisher wishes to thank The Kennel Club and The American
Kennel Club for permission to reproduce the breed standards.*

First published in Great Britain 1977 by
JOHN BARTHOLOMEW & SON LIMITED
12 Duncan Street, Edinburgh EH9 1TA
And at 216 High Street, Bromley BR1 1PW

John Bartholomew & Son Limited, 1977

ISBN 0 7028 1044 4

1st edition

Prepared for the Publisher by Youé & Spooner Ltd.
Colour illustrations by Graham Dorsett; airbrush drawings by Malcolm Ward

Printed in Great Britain by John Bartholomew & Son Limited

Preface

The German Shepherd or Alsatian is one of the best known and respected breeds in the world. This animal can fairly claim to be the most versatile dog of all and is also possibly the most misunderstood. The author of this book has known and loved the breed all her life and has had considerable experience of both the companion and the working dog. Being one of the most intelligent of all breeds, the German Shepherd can be one of the most rewarding of family pets. Mrs. Ixer explains the history, temperament and training that will enable you to appreciate the fine qualities of the German Shepherd and also enable you to get the best from your dog. As well as general care, details of breeding and exhibiting are given for the novice owner. This book is a great tribute to a breed that is the most widely known and kept throughout the world.

Wendy Boorer
Consultant Editor

The German Shepherd Dog in a traditional rôle

Breed history

The present-day Alsatian (German Shepherd Dog) does not have a very long history as a separate breed. It was only in the 1880s that an effort was made in Germany to fix a special type of sheep-dog from the many kinds then in use, which had been developed over many, many years, to work sheep there. Previously they varied in size, in coat and in ear carriage, and no doubt in temperament, but they had to work with sheep or they would not have been kept. So never, ever forget that the German Shepherd has a history as a working sheep-dog before being bred to a standard type. It is first and foremost a working dog. As a companion dog it is not always using all its inherited capabilities.

The type of dog developed was one to suit the conditions under which it had to work. It had to be big enough but not too heavy and it had to be able to move quickly. It had to be alert, trainable and above all of high intelligence as this dog not only had to work sheep to its master's commands, it was also expected to think for itself if left in charge of the flock when on pastures without fencing. For this reason we call the breed the German Shepherd, not the German Sheep-dog.

A clever dog working sheep is always an attractive sight and sheep-dog trials are very popular with the public. What a pity we do not see the German Shepherd working sheep in this country or have sheep-dog trials for the breed as they still do in Germany.

Just think of all a shepherd dog would be required to do in its work. It would have to cover miles at a steady trot, but be ready to break into a gallop or turn quickly when necessary. It must be able to stand up to a ram or a ewe with lamb which might defy it, but must not get over-excited or noisy enough to upset the sheep, which need intelligent handling or they easily panic. Neither must it bite at the sheep.

Of course, not all members of the breed come up to the standard required but the German Shepherd at its best can carry out all these tasks, and these inherited traits can be used for other purposes. Thus you have your police dogs, developed from the flock-guarding instincts and fearlessness of the shepherd dog which can still be expected to be friendly when off duty. This switch on and off quality is typical of the breed and often not understood. You also have your gentle,

Points of the German Shepherd Dog

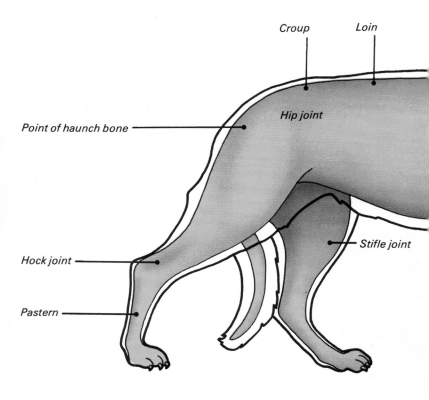

Croup

Loin

Point of haunch bone

Hip joint

Stifle joint

Hock joint

Pastern

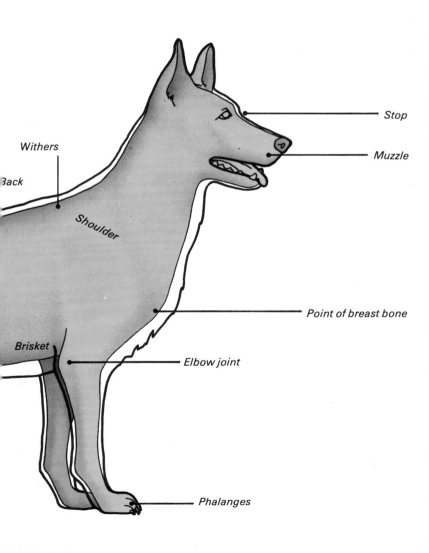

Stop

Muzzle

Withers

Back

Shoulder

Point of breast bone

Brisket

Elbow joint

Phalanges

steady guide dog for the blind which is probably the highest form of duty the breed can perform. Here the dog learns to think for another and to be the eyes of its master.

In between, there are all the other purposes for which this wonderful breed has been used, but only as a working sheep-dog can it develop fully the potential it was bred for. The breed was seldom seen in Britain before the 1914-18 war, but the troops, having seen the variety of work that it was trained to do by the Germans, such as carrying messages, laying wire, as well as working with the Red Cross, and as guard dogs, introduced some into this country soon after the war.

In 1910 the Club for German Shepherd Dogs (Verein für Deutsche Schäferhunde) had been formed in Germany and is still functioning today, and is usually referred to as the SV. It laid down the Standard, and rules the breed in a way that is not likely to be seen in Britain. Surveys called *Koerungs,* are held by specially appointed *Koerung* masters, where dogs brought for inspection are given marks for many points and graded accordingly. Attempts have been made to bring this system into Britain but it is not a popular idea. This is partly due to the system not being properly understood. Anyway the Standard the SV adopted, produced, by 1914, the German Shepherd of today or certainly a recognisable form of it.

As soon as they were seen in Britain, they attracted a great deal of attention but, when it came to registering the breed with the Kennel Club, it was felt that anything German in name would not be acceptable so, to the great detriment of the breed, it was decided to call them *Alsatian* Wolf Dogs. Why? Well, some had perhaps come from Alsace and it was in the right direction. (Please note that they are AlsatiAns not AlsatiOns as is so often printed.) Why Wolf Dogs? Well, they did have the look of a wolf and some were grey in colour, but this misnomer was to have a very bad effect on the general public. Some people took it to mean that the breed was a wolf-cross and not be trusted, and this, although not true, is still heard today. The wolf part of the title was dropped fairly soon but the damage had been done. Just think of the different image called to mind by the title 'wolf dog' instead of 'sheep-dog'.

Later, the proper name German Shepherd Dog was added in brackets, after Alsatian, and this is still the official title with the British Kennel Club and should appear on all pedigrees.

Editor's note. From this point on the breed will be referred to as the German Shepherd for consistency of nomenclature.

Attempts have been made to get the name changed to German Shepherd Dog but, even after a referendum held in 1975, which was overwhelmingly in favour, the Kennel Club turned it down. Thus Britain is almost the only country in the world where dogs of this breed are called Alsatians. It must be understood, however, that Alsatians and German Shepherds are the same breed. German Shepherds are *not* the long-coated variety as some people seem to think. Long coats are a fault in the breed.

In any case, whatever it was called, the breed had a rapid rise in numbers fifty years ago, and of course the quality of the stock and the temperaments suffered as a result of indiscriminate breeding to satisfy the demand. Incidents, however slight, of 'Wolf Dogs' attacking people became news and anything the poor German Shepherd does wrong is sure to be reported even today. I wonder if it would have been so if it had been called the German Shepherd?

As a result of the bad publicity and the poor specimens around, numbers fell. Dedicated breeders carried on breeding sound stock until the outbreak of the Second World War in 1939 when there was an appeal for suitable dogs and trainers to work with the Forces. A Government Guard Dog school was formed from those enlisted, which trained dogs and handlers to work with the Forces and Civil Defence. Here the good work done by these dogs in saving the lives of people buried by bombing helped to renew their popularity and the breed grew numerically again.

In fact, the number rose so much that the breed became the one with the most registrations at the Kennel Club for a time. In 1970 the number registered in Britain was 16,834.

This popularity, coupled with a demand for guard dogs, was to cause indiscriminate breeding again and once more the quality of the stock, but especially the temperament, suffered. The National Breed clubs have had to work hard to counter the adverse publicity resulting from this deterioration. Despite this set-back, the underlying qualities of the breed will always make it the only one for many devoted owners all over the world.

It is popular in most countries, many of which import their stock from Britain as well as from Germany. Australia did not allow any breeding stock into the country until a few years ago, but since the ban was lifted, they too have imported many dogs and bitches. As the breed comes from Germany, Britain has continually imported stock from there, especially when the breed was not numerically large, as new blood had to be brought in from time to time. Over the last few years imports have increased and since all the facts are available about German Dogs, due to their grading system and records, these imports should be useful in correcting the faults in the breed. However, the idea that everything German is either all good or not, as the case may be, is not to be encouraged. They should all be German Shepherd Dogs, wherever they are, bred to the same Standard.

There is now a World Union of German Shepherd Dogs' Clubs (WUSV) to which societies from all over the world can apply to belong. A meeting is arranged in Germany each year at which matters of interest to the breed as a whole are discussed. This is held shortly after the big German show, the *Sieger,* to which many people travel annually to see the huge classes judged under German rules and conditions.

The breed standard

What distinguishes the German Shepherd from other dogs, so that you can recognise a member of the breed from a distance? The head, the size and general outline should be enough. These important points are defined in the Standard for the breed along with the other characteristics that go to make it the working dog that it should be.

When the German Shepherd first came to Britain, to be recognised by the Kennel Club the breed had to have an approved Standard. This was drawn up using a translation from the German Standard, a very responsible task for those who prepared it. As well as a description of the dog's 'looks' which can be supplemented by illustrations, it was necessary to describe its character and temperament and its 'gait'. For a dog to work tirelessly, a sound, steady gait at all speeds is a necessity and a long-reaching trot is an attractive feature of the breed. This is not easy to describe, for it has to be seen to be believed. While the correct structure needed to produce this movement is detailed, movement is not so fully described in the British Standard as in the American one.

Under 'characteristics' it is felt by many that the choice of the word 'suspicious' is open to too many interpretations and the word 'aloof' would have been far better.

This breed should not be everybody's friend on sight. At home the dog has or should have its 'flock' to consider before it makes friends. It should not be either aggressive or shy. Off duty, and this means away from home or when its master takes over, the dog should be prepared to be friendly on investigation, and should not back away, barking. On a lead or under its master's control it should be at ease at once as its 'boss' has taken over and the dog should accept this and trust him. It is the nervous dog thinking only of its own skin that will never be a safe animal. Even if it is not a 'fear biter' (and not all nervous dogs are), it is a potential danger if it is likely to run away when startled and perhaps get run over or cause a bad accident.

Unfortunately, there is no requirement for a dog to pass a test of temperament and intelligence of any sort as a show dog. Some judges will try to see that a dog is not shy or nervous, but this is not fully possible in the ring, so that it is really in the hands of the breeder to see that the stock he breeds has the correct temperament. It is a great pity for the breed that a temperament test was not instituted right at the beginning, as this is a working breed first and foremost.

Efforts have been made from time to time to introduce a suitable test but it is doubtful if it will ever be possible to agree about it now. There is an unfortunate division between the show dog and the working dog, which is becoming ever harder to bridge. It is only fair to state that time is a big factor, 'showing' or 'working', each takes a lot of time and few people can combine the two these days. It is a great pity for the breed that we no longer have dual champions (i.e. for Breed and Obedience) let alone a working Trials and Breed Champion.

It is impossible to describe satisfactorily the intelligence and wonderful character of this breed. Those who have owned them for many, many years are still amazed at times at the way they think and behave. The American Standard for the Breed is more detailed than the British and is therefore printed as well for guidance. Since the German Standard must obviously be translated for those who do not speak German, and such translations vary, it is not discussed here but, for those who wish, it can be obtained from the SV.

The British Breed Standard

Characteristics *The characteristic expression of the Alsatian gives the impression of perpetual vigilance, fidelity, liveliness and watchfulness, alert to every sight and sound, with nothing escaping attention: fearless, but with decided suspiciousness of strangers — as opposed to the immediate friendliness of some breeds. The Alsatian possesses highly developed senses, mentally and temperamentally. He should be strongly individualistic and possess a high standard of intelligence. Three of the most outstanding traits are incorruptibility, discernment and ability to reason.*

General Appearance *The general appearance of the Alsatian is a well-proportioned dog showing great suppleness of limb, neither massive nor heavy, but at the same time free from any suggestion of weediness. It must not approach the greyhound type. The body is rather long, strongly boned, with plenty of muscle, obviously capable of endurance of speed and of quick and sudden movement. The gait should be supple, smooth and long-reaching, carrying the body along with the minimum of up-and-down movement, entirely free from stiltiness.*

Skeleton of the German Shepherd Dog

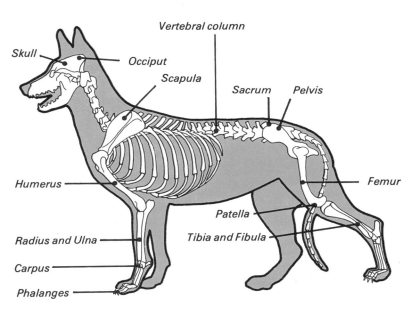

Head and Skull *The head is proportionate to the size of the body, long, lean and clean cut, broad at the back of the skull, but without coarseness, tapering to the nose with only a slight stop between the eyes. The skull is slightly domed and the top of the nose should be parallel to the forehead. The cheeks must not be full or in any way prominent and the whole head, when viewed from the top, should be much in the form of a V well filled in under the eyes. There should be plenty of substance in foreface, with a good depth from top to bottom. The muzzle is strong and long and, while tapering to the nose, it must not be carried to such an extreme as to give the appearance of being overshot. It must not show any weakness, or be snipy or lippy. The lips must be tight fitting and clean. The nose must be black.*

Eyes *The eyes are almond-shaped as nearly as possible*

matching the surrounding coat but darker rather than lighter in shade and placed to look straight forward. They must not be in any way bulging or prominent, and must show a lively, alert and highly intelligent expression.

Ears The ears should be of moderate size, but rather large than small, broad at the base and pointed at the tips, placed rather high on the skull and carried erect – in adding to the alert expression of the dog as a whole. (It should be noted, in case novice breeders may be misled, that in Alsatian puppies the ears often hang until the age of six months and sometimes longer, becoming erect with the replacement of the milk teeth.)

Mouth The teeth should be sound and strong, gripping with a scissor-like action, the lower incisors just behind, but touching the upper.

Neck The neck should be strong, fairly long with plenty of muscle, fitting gracefully into the body, joining the head without sharp angles and free from throatiness.

Forequarters The shoulders should slope well back, the ideal being that a line drawn through the centre of the shoulder blade should form a right-angle with the humerus when the leg is perpendicular to the ground in stance. Upright shoulders are a major fault. They should show plenty of muscle, which is distinct from, and must not be confused with, coarse or loaded bone, which is a fault. The shoulder-bone should be clean. The forelegs should be perfectly straight viewed from the front, but the pasterns should show a slight angle with the forearm when regarded from the side, too great an angle denotes weakness, and while carrying plenty of bone, it should be of good quality. Anything approaching the massive bone of the Newfoundland, for example, being a decided fault.

Body The body is muscular, the back is broadish and straight, strongly boned and well developed. The belly shows a waist without being tucked up. There should be a good depth of brisket or chest, the latter should not be too broad. The sides are flat compared to some breeds, and while the dog must not be barrel ribbed, it must not be so flat as to be actually slabsided. The Alsatian should be quick in movement and speedy but not like a greyhound in body.

Hindquarters The hindquarters should show breadth and strength, the loins being broad and strong, the rump rather long and sloping and the legs, when viewed from behind, must be quite straight, without any tendency to cow-hocks, or bow-hocks, which are both extremely serious faults. The stifles are well turned and the hocks strong and well let down. The ability to turn quickly is a necessary asset to the Alsatian, and this can only be if there is good length of thigh-bone and leg, and by the bending of the hock.

Feet The feet should be round, the toes strong, slightly arched and held close together. The pads should be firm, the nails short and strong. Dewclaws are neither a fault nor a virtue, but should be removed from the hind legs at four to five days old, as they are liable to spoil the gait.

Tail When at rest the tail should hang in a slight curve, and reach at least as far back as the hock. During movement and excitement it will be raised, but in no circumstances should the tail be carried past a vertical line drawn through the root.

Coat The coat is smooth, but it is at the same time a double coat. The undercoat is woolly in texture, thick and close and to it the animal owes its characteristic resistance to cold. The outercoat is also close, each hair straight, hard, and lying flat, so that it is rain-resisting. Under the body, to behind the legs, the coat is longer and forms near the thigh a mild form of breeching. On the head (including the inside of the ears), to the front of the legs and feet, the hair is short. Along the neck it is longer and thicker, and in winter approaches a form of ruff. A coat either too long or too short is a fault. As an average, the hairs in the back should be 1-2in. (2.5-5cm.) in length.

Colour The colour of the Alsatian is in itself not important and has no effect on the character of the dog or in its fitness for work and should be a secondary consideration for that reason. All white or near white unless possessing black points are not desirable. The final colour of a young dog can only be ascertained when the outer coat has developed.

Weight and Size The ideal height (measured to the highest point of the shoulder) is 22-24in. (56-61cm.) for bitches and 24-26in. (61-66cm.) for dogs. The proportion, of length to height, may vary between 10:9 and 10:8.5.

Faults A long, narrow, Collie or Borzoi head. A pink or liver-coloured nose. Undershot or overshot mouth. Tail with curl or pronounced hook. The lack of heavy undercoat.

The American Breed Standard

General Appearance The first impression of a good German Shepherd Dog is that of a strong, agile, well-muscled animal, alert and full of life. It is well balanced, with harmonious

 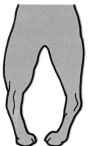 

Cow-hocked   *Barrel-legged*   *Broad*

Faults in hind legs

Barrel-legged   *Knock kneed*   *Narrow*

Faults in front legs

Faulty ear carriage

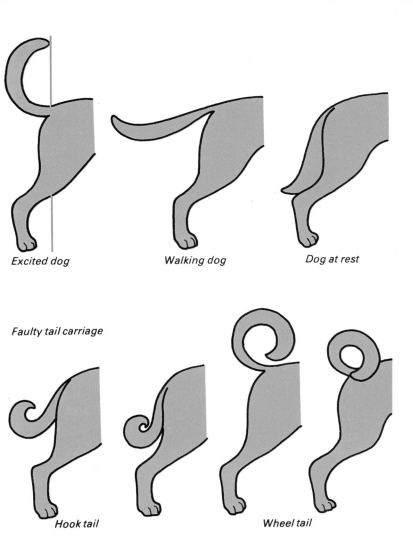

Excited dog

Walking dog

Dog at rest

Faulty tail carriage

Hook tail

Wheel tail

19

development of the forequarter and hindquarter. The dog is longer than tall, deep-bodied, and presents an outline of smooth curves rather than angles. It looks substantial and not spindly, giving the impression, both at rest and in motion, of muscular fitness and nimbleness without any look of clumsiness or soft living. The ideal dog is stamped with a look of quality and nobility — difficult to define, but unmistakable when present. Secondary sex characteristics are strongly marked, and every animal gives a definite impression of masculinity or femininity, according to its sex.

Character The breed has a distinct personality marked by direct and fearless, but not hostile, expression, self-confidence, and a certain aloofness that does not lend itself to immediate and indiscriminate friendships. The dog must be approachable, quietly standing its ground and showing confidence and willingness to meet overtures without itself making them. It is poised, but when the occasion demands, eager and alert; both fit and willing to serve in its capacity as companion, watch-dog, blind leader, herding dog, or guardian, whichever the circumstances may demand. The dog must not be timid, shrinking behind its master or handler; it should not be nervous, looking about or upward with anxious expression or showing nervous reactions, such as tucking of tail, to strange sounds or sights. Lack of confidence under any surroundings is not typical of good character. Any of the above deficiencies in character which indicate shyness must be penalized as very serious faults. It must be possible for the judge to observe the teeth and to determine that both testicles are descended. Any dog that attempts to bite the judge must be disqualified. The ideal dog is a working animal with an incorruptible character combined with body and gait suitable for the arduous work which constitutes its primary purpose.

Head The head is noble, cleanly chiseled, strong without coarseness, but above all not fine, and in proportion to the body. The head of the male is distinctly masculine, and that of the bitch distinctly feminine. The muzzle is long and strong with the lips firmly fitted, and its top line is parallel to the top line of the skull. Seen from the front, the forehead is only moderately arched, and the skull slopes into the long, wedge-shaped muzzle without abrupt stop. Jaws are strongly developed. **Ears** Ears are moderately pointed, in proportion to the skull, open toward the front, and carried erect when at

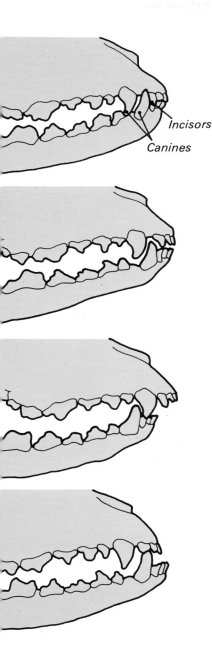

The correct 'scissors bite'. The upper incisors fit closely over the lower incisors and the upper canines fit behind the lower canines.

Incisors

Canines

'Pincer' or 'Level bite'. Teeth of the upper jaw meet the teeth of the lower jaw.

'Overshot'. The top jaw protrudes over the lower, causing a space. The canines are in reverse positions.

'Undershot'. The lower incisors protrude beyond the upper jaw, causing a space between the upper and lower canines.

attention, the ideal carriage being one in which the center lines of the ears, viewed from the front, are parallel to each other and perpendicular to the ground. A dog with cropped or hanging ears must be disqualified. **Eyes** Of medium size, almond-shaped, set a little obliquely and not protruding. The color as dark as possible. The expression keen, intelligent and composed. **Teeth** 42 in number – 20 upper and 22 lower – are strongly developed and meet in a scissors bite in which part of

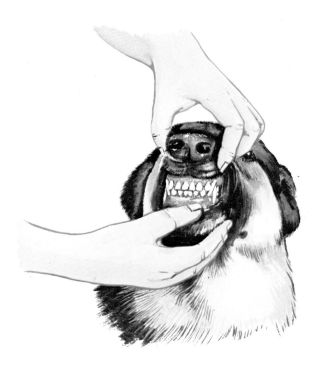

The teeth of a German Shepherd Dog showing the correct bite

the inner surface of the upper incisors meet and engage part of the outer surface of the lower incisors. An overshot jaw or a level bite is undesirable. An undershot jaw is a disqualifying fault. Complete dentition is to be preferred. Any missing teeth other than first premolars is a serious fault.

Neck The neck is strong and muscular, clean-cut and relatively long, proportionate in size to the head and without loose folds of skin. When the dog is at attention or excited, the head is raised and the neck carried high; otherwise typical carriage of the head is forward rather than up and but little higher than the top of the shoulders, particularly in motion.

Forequarters The shoulder blades are long and obliquely angled, laid on flat and not placed forward. The upper arm joins the shoulder blade at about a right angle. Both the upper arm and the shoulder blade are well muscled. The forelegs, viewed from all sides, are straight and the bone oval rather than round. The pasterns are strong and springy and angulated at approximately a 25° angle from the vertical.

Feet The feet are short, compact, with toes well arched, pads thick and firm, nails short and dark. The dewclaws, if any, should be removed from the hind legs. Dewclaws on the forelegs may be removed, but are normally left on.

Proportion The German Shepherd Dog is longer than tall, with the most desirable proportion as 10 to 8½. The desired height for males at the top of the highest point of the shoulder blade is 24-26in. (61-66cm.); and for bitches, 22-24in. (56-61cm.). The length is measured from the point of the prosternum or breastbone to the rear edge of the pelvis, the ischial tuberosity.

Body The whole structure of the body gives an impression of depth and solidity without bulkiness. **Chest** Commencing at the prosternum, is well filled and carried well down between the legs. It is deep and capacious, never shallow, with ample room for lungs and heart, carried well forward, with the prosternum showing ahead of the shoulder in profile. **Ribs** Well sprung and long, neither barrel-shaped nor too flat, and carried down to a sternum which reaches to the elbows. Correct ribbing allows the elbows to move back freely when the dog is at a trot. Too round causes interference and throws the elbows out; too flat or short causes pinched elbows. Ribbing is carried well back so that the loin is relatively short. **Abdomen** Firmly held and not paunchy. The bottom line is only moderately tucked up in the loin.

Ch. Commisar of Antolan (Ch. Ramacon Swashbuckler – Wraith of Hilrada)
Owned and bred by Mr. B. Hulme

Ch. Shootersway Xanthos of Colgay (Int. Ch. Druidswood Consort –
Shootersway Eurydice).
Owned by Mr. R. Collier, bred by Mr. and Mrs. Allan

Ch. Dermark Kari (English and N.Z. Champion Rossfort Premonition —
Octavia of Royden)
Owned and bred by Mr. and Mrs. D. Fenton

Ch. Tramella's Honddu Bechan (Clintonville Milord — Honddu Sasha)
Owned by Mr. and Mrs. J. Brough, bred by Mr. B. Stockwell

Topline : Withers *The withers are higher than and sloping into the level back.* **Back** *The back is straight, very strongly developed without sag or roach, and relatively short. The desirable long proportion is not derived from a long back, but from over-all length with relation to height, which is achieved by length of forequarter and length of withers and hindquarters viewed from the side.* **Loin** *Viewed from the top, broad and strong. Undue length between the last rib and the thigh, when viewed from the side, is undesirable.* **Croup** *Long and gradually sloping.* **Tail** *Bushy, with the last vertebra extended at least to the hock joint. It is set smoothly into the croup and low rather than high. At rest, the tail hangs in a slight curve like a sabre. A slight hook, sometimes carried to one side, is faulty only to the extent that it mars general appearance. When the dog is excited or in motion, the curve is accentuated and the tail raised, but it should never be curled forward beyond a vertical line. Tails too short, or with clumpy ends due to ankylosis, are serious faults. A dog with a docked tail must be disqualified.*

Hindquarters *The whole assembly of the thigh, viewed from the side, is broad, with both upper and lower thigh well muscled, forming as nearly as possible a right angle. The upper thigh bone parallels the shoulder blade while the lower thigh bone parallels the upper arm. The metatarsus (the unit between the hock joint and the foot) is short, strong and tightly articulated.*

Gait *A German Shepherd Dog is a trotting dog, and its structure has been developed to meet the requirements of its work.* **General Impression** *The gait is outreaching, elastic, seemingly without effort, smooth and rhythmic, covering the maximum amount of ground with the minimum number of steps. At a walk it covers a great deal of ground, with long stride of both legs and forelegs. At a trot the dog covers still more ground with even longer stride, and moves powerfully but easily, with co-ordination and balance so that the gait appears to be the steady motion of a well-lubricated machine. The feet travel close to the ground on both forward reach and backward push. In order to achieve ideal movement of this kind, there must be good muscular development and ligamentation. The hindquarters deliver, through the back, a powerful forward thrust which slightly lifts the whole animal and drives the body forward. Reaching far under, and passing*

A White German Shepherd Dog can make a fine pet, but will not be suitable for showing

A black German Shepherd Dog

the imprint left by the front foot, the hind foot takes hold of the ground; then hock, stifle and upper thigh come into play and sweep back, the stroke of the hind leg finishing with the foot still close to the ground in a smooth follow-through. The over-reach of the hindquarter usually necessitates one hind foot passing outside and the other hind foot passing inside the tack of the forefeet, and such action is not faulty unless the locomotion is crabwise with the dog's body sideways out of the normal straight line. **Transmission** The typical smooth, flowing gait is maintained with great strength and firmness of back. The whole effort of the hindquarter is transmitted to the forequarter through the loin, back and withers. At full trot, the back must remain firm and level without sway, roll, whip or roach. Unlevel topline with withers lower than the hip is a fault. To compensate for the forward motion imparted by the hindquarters, the shoulder should open to its full extent. The forelegs should reach out close to the ground in a long stride in harmony with that of the hindquarters. The dog does not track on widely separated parallel lines, but brings the feet inward toward the middle line of the body when trotting in order to maintain balance. The feet track closely but do not strike nor cross over. Viewed from the front, the front legs function from the shoulder joint to the pad in a straight line. Viewed from the rear, the hind legs function from the hip joint to the pad in a straight line. Faults of gait, whether from front, rear or side, are to be considered very serious faults.

Color The German Shepherd Dog varies in color and most colors are permissible. Strong rich colors are preferred. Nose black. Pale, washed-out colors and blues and livers are serious faults. A white dog or a dog with a nose that is not predominantly black, must be disqualified.

Coat The ideal dog has a double coat of medium length. The outer coat should be as dense as possible, hair straight, harsh and lying close to the body. A slightly wavy outer coat, often of wiry texture, is permissible. The head, including the inner ear and foreface, and the legs and paws are covered with short hair, and the neck with longer and thicker hair. The rear of the forelegs and hind legs has somewhat longer hair extending to the pastern and hock, respectively. Faults in coat include soft, silky, too long outer coat, woolly, curly, and open coat.

Choosing a puppy

When you have decided that a German Shepherd is the only breed you want, how do you obtain a suitable puppy? Since you are buying a companion for some years to come, it does not pay to be in too great a hurry. Do not rush out and buy the first puppy that you can find for sale without any thought beforehand of what you are taking on. Worse still, do not answer an advertisement and have a puppy sent unseen. This can only lead to disappointment.

With a breed as numerically large as the German Shepherd, it should not be too difficult to find a breeder near enough to visit. There are many breed clubs throughout the world and the secretaries of these will be glad to put you in touch with local breeders. Your Kennel Club can furnish you with breed club addresses.

The breed clubs can be of great help to the would-be owner. Contact the Secretary and tell him what you are looking for and he will most likely be able to give you the addresses of kennels that will have puppies for you to see. Please make an appointment before you visit kennels. Breeders are busy people so while they will be pleased to discuss their stock at convenient times, if you find that you cannot keep the appointment ring up to say so to avoid anyone waiting about for you. It is only polite to do so.

From what you have read and know of the breed, you will realise that here is a very interesting and versatile dog, capable of working well in a variety of ways, with a great potential for training to do many useful tasks. Therefore, if given the chance, it will become a really worthwhile companion or family dog. You will also realise that in certain strains one or other of the breed's characteristics are likely to have been more highly developed. For instance, some kennels breed for working dogs likely to be accepted for training by the police, others hope that they will have a puppy which will pass the tests and be trained to be a guide dog for the blind, but most kennels are developed with the hope of breeding winners in the show ring. It is hoped that these breeders accept the responsibility of keeping the correct temperament and character of a working breed.

It should always be possible to buy a puppy from a show bred litter and train it for any work, but the likelihood of this

being so is not so great as it used to be. This does not mean that you will not find your companion dog at a show breeding kennels. But it does mean that you should take care to see the parents of the pups.

If you want a good-looking, companion dog then surely its parents should possess these characteristics. That is, they should be dogs capable of leading a family life. I will never believe that the German Shepherd is a dog to be kept all the time in kennels. To be at its best, it needs to be doing a job and this can be looking after its family and joining in their lives. Most small kennels have realised this and have kept their numbers low enough for all the dogs to have at least some time in the house and for some to live all the time as house dogs. So do see that the dam of your pups is at home in the house under the sort of conditions that you expect to keep your dog. She will have a great deal of influence on the litter in the first few weeks and, although puppies are adaptable to their

The German Shepherd Dog is widely used for police and tracking work

surroundings when you get them young, a good start is essential.

All show breeders will have surplus stock to sell, and they will want to have satisfied clients in order to maintain a good reputation. This will not be the case if they breed nervous or unsound dogs. So do not be afraid to approach a show kennel for a companion dog, as you will be getting the benefit of experience in breeding and rearing, but do see that the dogs are socialised – not kept solely as kennel dogs.

When you visit a kennels, all the dogs and bitches should be pleased to see you and to make friends after an initial inspection. You will hope to meet some loose around the house or grounds and any dogs that you are shown in runs should also greet you happily and without too much barking.

When you have decided on a kennel that has dogs that you like, you may find that you can choose a puppy from a litter ready to leave or you may have to wait to get the one you want.

If you go to see the pups in the nest before they are ready, do not expect to see the bitch with them. She may not like visitors at this time, which is only natural. Her instincts to guard her puppies may become uppermost early on but by the time the pups are ready to go, although she will not be looking her best, she should now be pleased to inspect you as the prospective owner of a puppy and to make friends.

The choice

Puppies that are ready to leave the litter should be active, alert and not in any way shy or retiring. Mostly at this age they run up to everyone for attention and this is what you want. They should be well grown and well boned but not too heavy and certainly not fat. Make sure that they have 'clean' coats, i.e. free from parasites or any skin trouble. The skin should be loose but puppies should feel 'solid' when picked up. Their legs may appear large and out of proportion but these and 'knobbly' knees will 'fine down' as they grow.

I am assuming that the breeder will not let you have the puppy before eight weeks old and at that age they should weigh about 15lb. (7kg.). Any dew claws present at birth on the hind legs should have been removed at a few days old, although they are left on the front legs in this breed.

Look carefully at their mouths to see that they are not overshot or undershot but that their teeth are likely to meet in a correct bite.

All puppies should have been correctly wormed by eight weeks old. If you want a veterinary certificate of health, then ask the breeder beforehand if you can have this provided by his veterinary surgeon. You will be taking the pup to your veterinary surgeon for inoculations against hardpad, etc. soon after you get it and you can have a general check up then, but puppies are not sold on approval and it is far better, if you do not trust your own judgment, to have an opinion before you take the puppy away.

Ears are not likely to be erect at this age. If they are then they may be small when adult. It is far better that they are only starting to 'move' and are 'all over the place'. Very large ears which look heavy and show no sign of movement are best avoided.

Dark eyes are to be recommended in the grown dog but it is rather a tricky problem to determine the final colour at this

early age. To be attractive when adult, the eyes need to be darker than the hair surrounding them and as a general rule yellowish eyes should be avoided even at the puppy stage.

If you are hoping to show your puppy, tell the breeder so, although it is not possible to pick a winner for certain at a very early age; some are more likely than others to make the grade. Pay attention to the way the puppy moves, as this is so important in the show ring. The correct formation will result in a sound, long-reaching gait from the start.

What you pay for your puppy will depend on the prices ruling at the time. Compare the various prices asked at different kennels and decide accordingly. Remember a cheap puppy is usually a dear buy in the long run.

Sex Should you buy a dog or a bitch? This will depend on your own likes and dislikes. At one time dogs were more popular because of the nuisance of bitches coming into season twice a

Shrinkage of black in coat colour on a black/gold

year but this does not seem to count so much these days. A dog will usually be harder to train, as, if it can, it will try to be the boss when it grows up, but some dogs of this breed, even if they do take more training, have wonderfully gentle natures.

Bitches are slightly smaller and more willing to please. They are not difficult when in season, few ever try to run away but of course they must be kept shut up or exercised well away from home when on heat, or you will have all the dogs in the neighbourhood around. If you have young children who are likely to open doors and let her out and you feel that you really want a bitch, then it is best to send her to kennels for this time.

If you are not wanting to breed from her she can be spayed so that she will not come into season or be bred from at all. This is something you will have to discuss with your veterinary surgeon. Some people feel that it is a sensible thing to do, others that it is not natural. You will have to watch the diet carefully of a spayed bitch or she will tend to get too fat.

I have never found that the operation changes the character of a bitch but I have not been able to accept the need to have a dog castrated because he is a nuisance after bitches. This, I think, needs far more careful thought before making such a decision.

Colour You may have a decided preference for a certain colour and so know what you are looking for but you must remember that a German Shepherd puppy is not born the colour it will be when adult. Puppies in any litter will usually have different markings, varying in the amount of black and the colour of the lighter markings, from tan through gold to fawn or cream. These markings will spread and brighten and the pup is going to look lighter when it has its adult coat. So be careful that you do not choose the lightest pup in the litter and so end up with one that is too pale. Only a bi-colour, which is nearly all black with just lighter markings on the legs, is going to stay the same. An experienced breeder will be able to point these out.

Otherwise the lighter colour can spread until it leaves only a black saddle, or even 'break' all over, when they are incorrectly called Golden Sables. These they are not. A sable is born sable and will have had at least one sable parent. As a puppy it will be fawn, grey or gold all over but will darken as it grows its top coat. Sables are not nearly as common as they once were. They are seldom seen in the show ring now and are not so popular with the general public. No one seems to know why.

All blacks are seen from time to time but are not very common, and all whites are not accepted for showing.

You will usually have a preference resulting from those that you have known and liked, but I do not think that colour will play all that important a part in deciding the pup you choose, which I hope will be the one that appeals to you. In fact it may choose you!

You may see a long-coated pup in the litter and they can be very attractive at this age. If you are not wanting to show, although its coat may need a little more attention, there is no reason to turn it down.

If you have to wait for your puppy to be old enough to leave the kennels where it was born, you will have time to get prepared for its arrival. Obtain a diet sheet from the breeder and order all the food it will require for the first few days. Also get a suitable box for a bed.

When you contact the Secretary of your nearest breed club, you should enquire what meetings or training sessions are held so that you can attend these yourself to learn more about the breed. You will be far more relaxed if you attend without a puppy, to get used to the routine, and you will be able to learn what is likely to be expected of you and your dog.

Even if you are not going to train for obedience competitions or shows, there is much to be learnt about general management, etc. by watching and discussing the breed with the other enthusiasts there. Later, your dog too will benefit from meeting other owners of the breed and, more important, other dogs. Those kept as 'only ones' can grow up to find it difficult to get on with their own kind, if they are not used to it from the start. If you are getting your pup at eight weeks, it will be some time before it can attend anyway, but if contact has already been made, any helpful advice needed will be available and you will have made friends who will want to come to see your puppy and assist you in any way that may be necessary.

Transaction

The great day arrives when you go to collect your puppy. Take plenty of newspaper as it may be sick in the car on the way home and do not forget your money to pay for it. It has been done in the excitement of the event. You will have been asked for a deposit when you booked your puppy but do remember

A sample pedigree certificate

that the balance is payable when you collect it.

Do not leave the kennels without a receipt and the puppy's pedigree. This will usually be of either four or five generations and it does not matter which. As well as the pedigree, which is an unofficial document, you will need to know that the litter has been registered with the Kennel Club. New regulations came into force in Britain on 1 April 1976, so that now the breeder has to register the litter as a whole within twenty-eight days of the birth. He will then receive application forms for each puppy to enable each one to be entered in the Basic Register.

The breeder can do this himself if he wishes to use his own prefix when naming the dog, and if this has been done, he will give you the registration certificate and a signed transfer form to send, with the fee, to the Kennel Club, to have the puppy transferred to your ownership. He may, however, leave the registration of the puppy to you and in this case will give you a signed registration form. You will then choose a name and send the form to the Kennel Club with the required fee. Please note that in this case you must not use the prefix of the breeder or that of anyone else.

If later you decide to show, breed or export any dog, then it will have to be advanced from the Basic Register to the Active Register and another form completed and sent to the Kennel Club.

So now you have your puppy at home. It may possibly have been sick in the car, although young puppies usually travel well, but everything will certainly be very strange to it. It may, however, have slept all the way and be ready to explore. Whatever you do, try to put the puppy down on the grass in a safe place before you take it indoors. It will quite likely perform and you can give your first praise! Anyway, keep talking to it and it will soon follow you about. Your voice will be both security and comfort.

Decide on a name for it as soon as you can, as it will quickly learn this and respond. Take the puppy indoors and relax. Do not be in a hurry to feed it. It may want a little drink but no more. Even though it will probably have missed a meal in order to travel 'safely', it is better left to settle. It will almost certainly trail around after you and do a certain amount of exploring as it begins to feel surer of itself and at home. Odds are that when you sit down for a meal it will settle to sleep on your feet. Do not worry about its bed at this stage; let sleeping dogs lie!

If it is a greedy type or is very hungry, it may not settle if it can smell your food and it may be necessary to give the puppy a small meal before it rests, but it is more likely that it will need a sleep after the journey and the first impressions of its new home.

When the pup awakes, *take it out* fast! It will probably 'go' without stopping to think and while still yawning. Praise it and you have started its training.

Now it should be ready for a meal but do not worry if it does not seem too hungry. You have the diet sheet given to you by the breeder but for the first forty-eight hours at least do not give the full amounts. The change in surroundings will be enough for it to cope with, but puppies are adaptable and will soon accept a new routine at this age.

If its digestion does get upset by the move, then go so far as to miss one meal and make the next one a light one, but if diarrhoea persists into a second day, then seek veterinary advice. Puppies digest their food so quickly and are growing so fast, that any upset should right itself quickly or it must be attended to.

If it does not want to eat, take the food away and make the next meal a little late. It is usually lack of competition from the rest of the litter plus all the exciting new happenings that interest it more than eating. Do be sure that you are not over-feeding it. It is so easy to pop a little extra in 'to do the puppy good', when it will do nothing of the sort.

Remember, too, that unless the breeder has fed each puppy separately, it will not be known exactly how much your puppy has been eating and the diet sheet will give only average amounts. Your puppy may have been getting more or less than this and it will take a day or so for you to find out its actual needs.

Now we come to the first night. Remember you have taken the pup away from its mother (who was probably fed up with it anyway), its kennel and its litter brothers and sisters, and plonked it down in a competely new situation, and you are its only known contact and likely source of comfort. Your voice is all it recognises and so far as I am concerned there is only one place for a puppy to sleep to start with and that is beside my bed in a tea chest or other deep box. Why? Simply because it then has the comfort of another living 'animal' near at hand and, equally important, it will wake you when and if it wants to go out.

Dogs do not dirty their beds if they can possibly help it and the puppy will whimper and try to climb out. Rush it outside and you are on the way to house training. You will of course have taken the trouble to go out with it before bedtime and stay long enough for it to get the message. Now hopefully you will have a peaceful night from the start and in a few days, the puppy will be sleeping through the night in a settled routine.

However, if you feel that you must start as you mean to go on, and the puppy has to sleep alone in the kitchen, ('deserted' it will consider it), then you must make it as comfortable as possible in its bed. Give the puppy a hot-water bottle for warmth, and I am told a ticking clock placed near will soothe it.

Put down plenty of paper near the door and hope for the best. The bed should be placed under a table or in a corner if possible to give the feeling of being more sheltered. Now go away and harden your heart because the puppy is going to cry for you. It is not natural for a puppy to be alone. They are born in litters, rarely singly, so you are expecting it to do something completely alien, in sleeping alone.

The puppy will accept it eventually but suffer in the process. This is not a case of starting as you mean to go on, as once the pup is settled and used to you and its home and sleeping in its bed in the daytime it will, if you wish, transfer to sleeping there at night.

No eight-week-old puppy should be expected to sleep alone in a kennel outside.

Rearing and general care

The first night over, the pup should be hungry for its breakfast as laid down in its diet sheet and then be ready to explore its new home more thoroughly and to settle in. Encourage it to use its bed in the daytime to sleep, in but it will most likely fall asleep anywhere to start with. Do not forget it is a baby, albeit an independent one in some ways. It needs your company to replace that of its brothers and sisters and it is during these first few weeks that you can develop a close relationship with your pup, which will last its lifetime.

It will trust you completely and rely on you not only to feed it but most of all for love and affection. In return it will try to please you to get your praise and attention and will know at once if you are displeased by the tone of your voice. The German Shepherd is a highly sensitive breed and can quickly learn from the start what is required of it. However, as with all dogs, the puppy can only be corrected for anything it does wrong if caught in the act and then merely 'told off' or scolded. Nothing more in the way of punishment is necessary.

To be 'clean' in the house is likely to be the first lesson to be learned and this is usually a very simple matter. From a few weeks old, the pups should have been accustomed to using one corner of their kennel or run by being put there after meals and when woken up. This part will be kept covered with newspapers or sawdust and not so scrupulously cleaned as the rest of the kennel. A slightly soiled newspaper or a little wet sawdust left behind when cleaning will see that the pups quickly learn that here is *the* place. You can carry on this habit by always taking it to the same spot in the garden after meals, when it wakes up and last thing at night. Then when the puppy performs correctly, see that it is praised.

Do not scold too much for the first few days if mistakes occur (it is probably your fault anyway), and then only if you catch the puppy in the act, when, as well as using a scolding voice, you take it to the spot where it should have been done. If it has to be left indoors longer than it is likely to be able to wait, for the first few weeks put newspapers or a tray of sawdust down in a convenient place (and remove all rugs). German Shepherds are very easy to house train and once trained they do not like to make a mistake.

From the start when putting the puppy out give a simple

command, such as 'hurry up', in an encouraging voice. Gradually you will be able to use this command in places other than the first spot chosen and you are well on the way to having a dog that will quickly relieve itself when the opportunity arises.

This is very useful when away from home, as most dogs (especially bitches) dislike using 'new' ground without thorough investigation and you haven't always the time to wait. The usual command will let them know it is in order to go there and bring about the conditioned response. This is very necessary if you are likely to be in towns or built-up areas where soiling the pavements is liable to result in a large fine. Your dog can be shown the gutter or other allowable spot and told that that is where it goes. It is not difficult to teach if you start young enough and it does make you more of a responsible citizen.

Now is the time to establish a routine. Remember, the puppy must have regular feeding times and, just as important, regular sleeping times. In between it will want 'amusing' at the times it would have played with its litter mates.

To begin with, this will consist mainly of following you about and of a short 'walk' in the garden. The puppy will not go out on

Puppy pen

43

a lead for a walk for a time yet, but it does need to become socialised and used to meeting people at this early age. Let it make as many friends as possible. It is hoped that you have a household where plenty of people come and go. If not, invite them while the puppy is young and especially introduce it to all the regular tradesmen who call, so that it will know that they are friends too. Although this is the age to let it get used to children, do not let them handle it too much, as they can so easily tire out a young puppy.

The pup will probably fall asleep when it is tired at this stage. It is a little later on that it may tend to keep on too long and then its rest times must be adhered to.

Remember to make arrangements with your veterinary surgeon for the puppy to have its inoculations at the required age against distemper, etc. as it cannot be taken out and about safely until these are completed.

Growing on
With the inoculations completed and your pup settled into a routine, you will be amazed at how fast it is growing and you will soon be wanting to see its ears go up. This may not happen permanently until it has finished teething but they should start

'to move' after a few weeks. A very few puppies will have one or both ears erect at eight weeks but, as has been stated, these are usually rather small ears. Puppies vary as to when their ears are erect and the shape of the ear has a lot to do with it. Do not get worried too soon, especially if they are moving about or if they are up one day and down the next. Once they have been up, they will almost certainly stay up eventually when teething is over.

A dog with 'soft' ears, as they are called if not erect, is not typical of the breed and will not win in the show ring. It is possible to 'tape' the ears up to help them stiffen but this must be done by an expert and at the proper time. You will need to seek the advice of the breeder if you are worried that the ears are not up as you think they should be.

Your puppy will start to lose its milk teeth and erupt its permanent ones at about four months old. Normally, apart from a desire to chew everything in sight, it will not suffer any discomfort but sometimes the gums get inflamed or the large canine teeth come through without the baby ones coming out. This should be watched for and veterinary advice sought. See that the pup has large bones or 'dog chews' to gnaw at and all should be well.

Occasionally pups get earache when teething but as any ear trouble may be serious the veterinary surgeon should be consulted.

Puppies vary as to the time it takes to get their permanent set of teeth through but they will probably have finished teething by nine months old.

The first six months are most important to this breed. They are growing fast and need careful feeding to maintain this growth. They must not get too fat nor must they have too much exercise, but they must get out and about and get used to family life. They must also have plenty of rest. As they get bigger it is easy to think of them as grown up but the German Shepherd is not fully mature until two years old.

Feeding

There are various suitable foods for dogs and although you are advised to keep to the diet sheet that you were given with the puppy, it may be necessary to change later on.

Twenty or so years ago there were just two main ways of feeding, either cooked meat with biscuit and gravy or raw meat with biscuits (or a separate cereal meal, soaked or dry). There were variations on this diet but the main thing to decide was whether to feed meat raw or cooked.

I would say that to cook meat and add biscuit has lost its popularity although still practised. Far more people now feed raw meat, some still with biscuit added but many with cereal as a separate meal.

Dogs are carnivores and need meat for their protein requirements and can, in fact, live well on a wholly meat diet. Naturally they would not eat the flesh that we tend to give them, preferring the offal and stomach contents first; they would also eat whole small mammals such as rabbits, skin and all. It is considered that dogs also need cereals as carbohydrates for energy, although if too much is fed they will become fat.

In the last few years a whole new range of 'complete' foods have been developed which are claimed to contain all that a dog needs for perfect health and growth. These foods just need to be fed in the correct amount, wet or dry, according to instructions. Many people find that these diets are excellent. They are fairly expensive but can be bought in bulk; they store well and are easy to feed, and you may well find that your puppy has been fed this way. If so, do keep closely to the maker's instructions as they vary from food to food. Do not change brands if the one you are using is satisfactory. When they are not giving satisfactory results these diets are mostly not being used properly. Often too much is being given.

Cooked meat with or without cereal is widely available in tins and is therefore a variety of the cooked meat diet that is easily obtainable. The best are usually the most expensive and worth it because they contain more meat. It is far better to add cereal to the all-meat variety.

Tinned meats are a very useful form of emergency rations and for taking on holiday, but it is still possible to find a source of fresh meat through pet food suppliers (consult the classified telephone directory), that will be better for your dog. Most pet food shops carry supplies of meat in blocks.

Puppies must be fed regularly and well. They grow very quickly during the first six months and poor feeding during this time can never be made up later. Little (of the best) and often should be the rule. Never over-feed or you will cause indigestion or worse. Meals should be taken at about

four-hourly intervals and gradually the evening meal increased to become the main meal of the day, so that the dog can rest after it.

By four months old your puppy is going to eat as much as when adult and may well eat more during the fast growing and developing stage up to one year or longer.

Suggested diet for an eight-week-old German Shepherd Dog
Four feeds a day

1 Breakfast	Two cupfuls of milk thickened with a heaped tablespoon of baby cereal or some breakfast cereal.
Or as 3 Tea	A small cup of soaked puppy biscuit meal moistened with milk. The biscuit should have been well soaked with boiling water and allowed to cool. Puppies like these feeds milky, not stodgy.
2 and 4 Lunch and Supper	8oz. (228g.) raw meat cut up very small with a little finely chopped vegetable (this can be cooked green vegetable to start with but finely grated raw vegetables such as carrot should be introduced as soon as possible).

A complete vitamin and mineral supplement should be fed daily as per instructions either as tablets or powder sprinkled on food. German Shepherds grow so fast that sterilised bone flour can with advantage be added to their diet for the first few months. Start with a level teaspoon and increase to a maximum of a level tablespoon once each day by six months old. This bone meal can be obtained from pet food shops. A raw egg should be given occasionally with the meat meal. A drink of milk can be given last thing at night for a few weeks until the pup has settled.

Increase the above amounts gradually week by week until at four months or so the amount of milk, biscuit meal and meat taken have been doubled. Only give as much as the puppy will eat straight away. Never leave food about, but remember the puppy is growing fast and its appetite should increase almost daily. By six months old only one cereal meal of soaked biscuit should be necessary and 'tea' omitted, and by one year old the amount of meat necessary can be taken at one meal. The adult diet then becomes a main meal at night of approximately 2lb. (1kg.) meat (with some vegetables) and a few biscuits or slices of dry wholemeal bread fed at a separate time.

If the dog has a tendency to get fat, the cereal feed should be cut down or even omitted for a time or charcoal biscuits substituted. The amount of food needed will vary with each individual and the amount of exercise taken. Milk is not necessary to the adult dog and even for puppies cows' milk is a very poor substitute for bitches' milk and should only be used until teething is completed. Goats' milk is nearer to bitches' in composition and should be used if obtainable. Dried milk powder of suitable formula for babies can be used if that prepared especially for puppies is not available.

See that fresh water is always available. Pups love to play in water so the bowl should be heavy enough not to be turned over easily and not big enough for the pup to get too much of itself into it. Some dogs are 'messy' drinkers, so place the bowl where it will not matter if a few drops get spilt and then keep it filled with clean water, frequently replaced.

A food bowl has been developed that has a wide enough circular mat attached to the bottom for the pup to put its paw on when eating; this steadies the bowl and it is not so likely to be turned over.

No cooked bones should ever be given. Large beef bones are usually safe and much enjoyed as well as being beneficial but these days the advice of your veterinary surgeon should be taken about feeding bones. Artificial 'chews' can now be obtained as chewing toys which will help teething and prevent the chewing of furniture, etc.

All dogs should have access to couch grass as a natural conditioner and if it is not available, then tablets of couch grass should be given regularly.

Grooming
Dogs love to be groomed and it is never too soon to start a gentle brushing of the coat. Teach your puppy to stand on a grooming table of suitable height so that you can handle it in comfort and it will soon be jumping up to wait for its daily session. The German Shepherd has an easy coat to look after.

When it is moulting its undercoat you will need a steel comb to strip it all out as quickly as possible and thus avoid having a 'tufty' looking dog. Otherwise, as well as the brush, use your hands. Wear gloves if you like, rubber ones are suitable, and with bent fingers extended as wide as is comfortable pull them

Puppy feeding at bowl on fixed mat

51

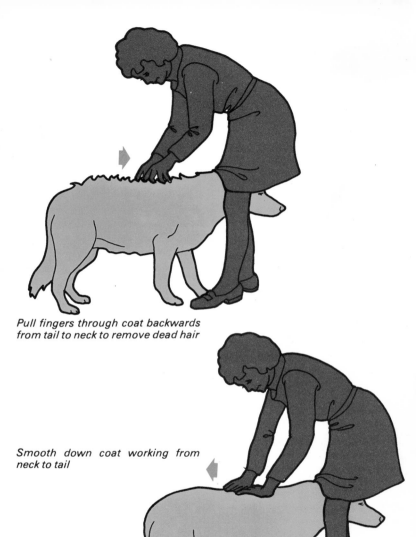

Pull fingers through coat backwards
from tail to neck to remove dead hair

Smooth down coat working from
neck to tail

52

through the coat backwards from tail to neck. Dogs love this 'combing' and it removes dead hair and stimulates growth.

Finally, smooth down with a grooming glove and although dogs vary as to how much shine they have on their coats, this grooming done frequently will make the most of the dog's coat.

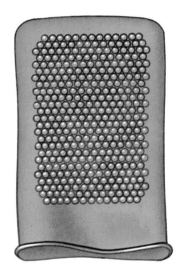

Rubber grooming glove

Steel rake for removing dead hair

It is seldom necessary to bath your German Shepherd unless it rolls in something unpleasant. For showing, a bath can make that extra difference but your house dog will look well without it. When moulting, a 'dry' or spray shampoo can help to remove the dead hair from a coat that looks dirty.

When grooming do look out for any extra 'livestock'. All dogs are liable to pick up fleas at times and will usually let you know by scratching, so see that these unwelcome visitors are removed by dusting with the correct powders, or a bath in a special shampoo may be necessary. Never let your dog scratch without finding out why and if it is fleas, then see that you replace all bedding as well.

Make sure that eyes and ears are cleaned regularly. Eyes should need only a wipe with damp cotton wool but be very gentle with ears, wiping them out with cotton wool dipped in a little olive or almond oil. If any soreness is present, or the dog scratches at its ears or shakes its head, then seek expert advice. Do not 'poke about' inside the ears; they are too sensitive.

Keep the toenails short, if possible with exercise on hard roads, but if they grow too long they will have to be trimmed by an expert. Once they have been cut it is usually necessary to have them done at regular intervals, as they then seem to grow again very quickly. Inexpert trimming can cut into the quick and cause the dog a great deal of pain.

See that the teeth are clean. Special toothpaste can be bought for dogs but chewing and gnawing at a bone will keep teeth clean naturally.

Exercise, training and showing

When adult the German Shepherd will be capable of taking more exercise than you can usually give but it is very adaptable. It is far better to keep to the amount you can manage daily, as long as it is enough to keep the dog healthy, than to give it a lot of exercise at the weekends and none during the week. Of course it likes extra walks at times but it is the regular daily walk that counts most. It can be basically the same each day if necessary. The dog will not mind and will be eager to find out what has taken place since the day before, as every walk is full of new, interesting smells. Dogs need a chance to romp and play with other dogs if possible, as well as to run free, and road work on a lead to keep their feet trim.

If being entered for a show, then the dog should be in tiptop condition, well muscled up and not in any way fat. To be shown in soft condition is a fault. To obtain this fitness, about five miles of moving at a steady trot is ideal and a bicycle will help here, if you can find a suitable place these days where it is quiet enough and safe to do so. Even in the country our roads are not as safe as they were. However, no German Shepherd should start to trot beside a bicycle before one year old and it must be slow enough for the dog to keep at the right pace.

Trotting beside a horse is an ideal form of exercise for German Shepherd Dogs. Given ten miles across country of this, to them gentle exercise, and they will be in fine fettle. Not many people can supply this form of exercise these days, so it is necessary to work out an amount that, while giving the dog sufficient for its needs, fits in with the daily routine.

More and more people seem to go about in cars, father to the station, children to school and mother shopping, etc. and, though the family dog enjoys this, it is not exercising him.

All the puppy needs until six months old is to run about in the garden, as too much exercise too soon can be very harmful to it. However, it will soon be old enough to start to go out and careful thought should have been given before this as to where it is suitable for the dog to be taken, and by whom. The daily exercise should not be a chore but willingly undertaken by one of the family, whatever the weather. German Shepherds are all-weather dogs and enjoy a run in the rain. They also enjoy swimming. They are quickly dried off on return, though a time on a deep bed of straw in a shed will help to clean them up.

Basic training

You start to train your puppy the first time you speak to it. Your voice is the key to its behaviour from that moment on. An experienced trainer will know almost instinctively how much 'voice' to use with each dog, as some will always need firmer treatment than others. Be the 'boss' of your dog, kindly, but firmly, from the start and you will have a happy, obedient dog who respects you. Dogs like discipline. They certainly get it under pack rule. Their 'mum' will have kept them in their place from the start, so it is up to you to follow on from the time you get your puppy.

Simple training should be part of its daily life, so that the dog grows up knowing what is required of it, and there will be no need for corrective treatment or punishment later. The new puppy is too young to have learned any bad habits but it is up to you to see that it gets the necessary attention while young so that it can learn what you want it to do.

You must be able to change the tone of your voice between giving commands, scolding or praising, and to say as few words as possible when giving commands. Talk as much as you like to your pup the rest of the time, but when training keep to the same few words and nothing else. Always start with the dog's name to get its attention, followed by a one-word command. See that the command is carried out, then praise the puppy. Just as the pup will be fed mainly by the person in the family responsible for its routine, so its basic training should be undertaken by the same person.

As the dog grows on and understands what is wanted, then it should be expected to obey basic commands from all members of the family, but it will only confuse a young pup if it is 'trained' by different people using different words and voices. While young, any training sessions should be very short. In fact, they are not really sessions at all, just a few minutes of conditioning at times when the puppy is likely to be responsive.

Come It is essential that your dog comes when it is called, so it is never too early to start a response to this command. Do keep to the one word *'come'* (not 'come here'), said in a firm but kind voice that tells the dog you mean it, not in a weak way that asks it to come if it feels like it.

At the start call its name *when it is already on its way towards you,* as puppies naturally do when they see you; add

Dog being recalled by handler

57

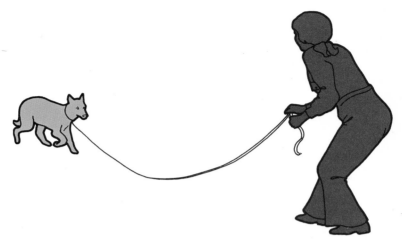

A long lead or line can be used to teach a reluctant dog to 'come' when recalled

A puppy can be taught to 'sit' in this way. Holding the food bowl at mealtimes you can gently push the hindquarters down

the command *'come'* and then make a real fuss of the dog when it arrives and tell it what a good dog it is. Keep this up for a few days and then you can try it when the puppy is not actually looking your way, but is not too interested in something else. Call its name in a happy, cheerful voice to get its attention, then when it looks in your direction, add the command *'come'* firmly. Clap your hands or your sides gently and the puppy should be running towards you to get the praise and fuss it has already learned to expect to receive when it reaches you.

This is conditioning that is going to stand you in good stead all the dog's life. Coming to you will become a fixed response to your voice and the command, and will be associated with pleasure. The test will come when there are other attractions about, but the more you fix this response at an early age, the more likely you are always to have an obedient dog.

If you are ignored, never chase the dog. Call it and then run the other way. If necessary hide behind something so that it has to look for you. Do not panic or shout. Keep your voice at its usual level. Your dog can hear you if it wants to and remember, when it does come, praise it, however long it takes to arrive. All this must, of course, be done in the garden at home while the pup is small and only put into practice elsewhere when these early lessons have been mastered.

Sit This is another command that can be taught early on. Your puppy will probably sit down to look up at you, especially when expecting its food and this is the time to teach the sit. With a dish or titbit in your hand, but held out of the dog's reach, say the pup's name and then the command *'sit'* (not 'sit down'). You may have to apply gentle pressure on the hindquarters to start with and be quick enough to stop the puppy jumping up, but it will soon learn what you want and this is a very useful command.

It is far better to give your dog the positive command to sit, if, with or without muddy feet, it looks like jumping up on people, than to keep on saying 'Down, down'. It can also be useful if the dog looks like chasing off. The simple command *'sit'* said as sharply as possible is more likely to get an automatic response. Then, when you have the dog's attention, you can call it in and praise it.

See that your dog enjoys obeying this command. Tell it to sit at odd times when it is running loose a short way from you and see that the dog sits where it is. Praise it and tell it to run free again. Gradually increase the distance from you at which the dog will sit on command. Do not let it come towards you before it obeys. Hand signals can be a help here. Raise your right arm straight above your head when giving the command.

Learning its place
It is essential that your puppy learns where it is to rest, so when it has been fed, taken out to be clean or is tired, it should be put in its bed and told *'place'*. It will be necessary to hold and stroke the puppy quietly to start with, or even to put it in a box that it cannot get out of, but it must learn its own place and that it goes there to sleep. Later you can take the bed or just a rug to another room and give the same command. Finally, you will have a dog that will stay quietly anywhere it is placed.

Once the puppy is settled with you in the house, it is essential that it learns to be left alone elsewhere. Of course, this must only be for a short time to start with. No one who is out all day should take on a puppy or an adult dog. German

A wicker basket bed

A metal framed canvas bed

Shepherds need to be with you to develop into sensible companions. However, there will be times when the dog must be left for a while and it is kindest to teach it this when young, by shutting it up in a shed or suitable kennel.

The dog will make a noise at first, but giving a firm command *'quiet'* and then leaving it and ignoring its barking or whining or other efforts to get out, will result in it settling down to rest undisturbed by any household distractions. Do not return to the dog while it is making a noise but do not leave it too long to start with. It must learn that it gets let out when it is quiet. It is better to put up with this noise at an early age than to wait until the dog is bigger and stronger physically and vocally.

This training is very necessary if you have a bitch who will have to be shut up when in season or if you are likely to have to send your dog to boarding kennels when you go away. Here it is suggested that you arrange with the boarding kennels to have your pup in for a day (or even half a day when you would like to go shopping), so that it knows what to expect when it is left later on. Most kennels have a slack period between holiday

Estate car fitted with dog guard

rushes and will welcome this idea if it means the dog will settle when you go away and leave it for a longer period.

Most dogs like car rides but for safety they should lie down quietly in the back. Fix a dog guard if possible to give a separate compartment, and have a passenger with you to see that the pup is made to behave from the start. It is not possible to drive safely and to correct a noisy or fidgety puppy at the same time.

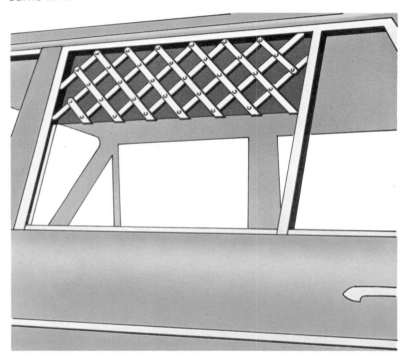

With a car parked in the shade, a trellis frame window vent can be used

Never leave a dog shut in a car if the weather is at all hot. Trellis frames can be obtained to fit over the windows to allow ventilation but cars heat up so quickly that a dog can be in distress from the heat in a very short time. Put a thermometer in the car and have a look at it when the car has been standing in the sun for a short while to see what can happen.

Stay When your puppy is sitting to command, then it is time to teach it to stay in that position until told to move. Make the length of time you expect it to sit very short to start with and when you release it, with a cheerful 'O.K' or some such phrase, see that you praise it. The *'stay'* must be said firmly and obeyed. Do not try for too long at a time so that you can always release the dog before it makes a move. Then you can praise not scold it.

Do remember that if you have to scold or show your displeasure with your dog at any time, you must 'make it up' with the animal immediately afterwards. Give a command that it enjoys obeying, just so that you can praise it again. Never try to train a dog if you are feeling irritable or out of sorts.

When your dog will stay in the sit position you will gradually be able to walk away a short distance, then to walk round it and finally, much later on, to go out of sight without it moving. Never, never call the dog to you if you have given the command to stay. It must stay until you return to tell it it may move. If it knows that you will always come back, it will trust you and stay.

Heel You can start training your puppy to walk to heel from a very early age by combining it with the *'come'* command. Occasionally as the pup runs towards you, just before it makes it, you turn round and walk on, patting your left side as you go. Adjust your pace to keep the puppy going in the heel position and give the command *'heel'* for a short way before stopping and praising it.

Later you will need a chain link collar and a long lead. This chain collar must be the correct length and weight for the size of the dog and be put on correctly so that it tightens only if the dog pulls but falls loose when the lead slackens. Never tie a dog up by a lead attached to a chain collar or let dogs with chain collars on play together. Dogs can choke before they can be released if the chain gets caught up on anything. However, properly used they are essential for training and controlling the dog.

To walk beside you on a lead without pulling may sound difficult to teach. Remember it takes two to pull, so do not let the dog pull you. Jerk the lead as soon as the dog goes too far forward and then release it when the dog is in the right place. Have the dog at your left side in the heel position with the lead held in your right hand. This leaves your left hand free to jerk

This is the correct way for a choke-chain to be when the dog is on your left side

the lead back, to pat your leg or to encourage the dog by any other method to keep with you.

Call the dog's name to get its attention, then say *'heel'*, and set off at a brisk pace in a cheerful manner. Almost run if necessary but see that your dog looks up at you and enjoys it. Once round the lawn is enough to start with. From now on you must gradually set the pace at which you want to walk but this must be at a suitable speed for the dog to keep up and not get bored.

A choke-chain

The puppy will not be going out for a walk on a lead until old enough, so you should have plenty of time to practise at home. If you can keep its attention on you, it will not try to pull ahead but you must walk fast enough to stop it jumping up or playing about. If the puppy goes ahead, jerk it back with the command *'heel'* but as soon as it is in the correct position, praise it and try to have a loose lead again.

Down, drop or flat It should not be difficult to make your puppy understand that you want it to lie down, as you can hold it in this position when it is small. It is, however, important to decide exactly what command you are going to give. *'Down'* and *'drop'* can mean other things, so make sure that the word you choose is used only when you wish the puppy to lie down. Avoid telling it to sit first and then to lie down, as this will slow up the response and mean giving two commands.

As soon as the puppy will go down by itself (and it is praised for so doing), start giving the *'stay'* command. The dog will have learned this in the 'sit' position, so there should be no difficulty in the 'down'. At the same time practise 'dropping' the dog at a distance from you, first on a long lead and then when loose. This should be a command that is instantly obeyed at any distance. As with the 'sit', a hand signal can help. Extend your right arm sideways level with your shoulder as you give the command.

Barking
Do not encourage a young puppy to bark at everything, for you will regret it later. The time for a dog to bark is when something strange is heard, not at every sound. It is essential that you can stop your dog barking when it is told. Persistent barking can be a cause of complaint from neighbours and, as German Shepherds are either loved or hated, seldom tolerated, you do not want to do anything that can cause annoyance. Your German Shepherd is too intelligent just to bark at anything. The dog should think before it acts.

Obedience Competitions and Working Trials
You may later decide that you would like to train your dog for Obedience Tests. If so, you should join a training club where you can learn the methods of training likely to help you to win. You and your dog can get a great deal of enjoyment out of this but it is a very competitive sport these days with very big entries in the early classes.

In Britain you may also have a Working Trials Society in your area and here your dog will have more scope to develop Tracking, Nosework and Agility.

Shows and showing
The showing of dogs can be a very interesting hobby but it is also taken very seriously by breeders and exhibitors who want to win prizes and so get their stock known to would-be purchasers.

Competition in the show ring is very keen in this breed, with large entries at most shows and, with only a few prizes awarded in each class, many good dogs will have to go without the 'red card' or first prize.

Even a potential champion will have to be groomed and handled to perfection if it is to win.

The real thrill will come when a dog that you have bred yourself leads the class and if achieved this will be worth all the

A working dog must be agile enough to jump and obedient enough to retrieve

68

hard work and expense involved.

Before buying any stock for show, go to as many shows as you can to see what it is like and to choose the type of winning dog that appeals to you. You can then approach the breeders of these dogs to see if they have any stock for sale. Buying a puppy to show when old enough is always taking a risk, as puppies can change so much while growing. The breeder will help you to pick out a possible winner but, although both parents may have done their share of winning, it will not guarantee that their offspring will do the same.

Exhibitors setting up their dogs in an outdoor show ring

You will have to decide if you are just going to local shows within easy reach or are prepared to travel about the country. The summer circuit of championship shows can involve buying many gallons of petrol if you are taking showing seriously.

In this case it is far better to buy a young dog or bitch of show standard, ready to be entered, or even one that has already won as a puppy. Although you will pay more, you will save yourself the disappointment of rearing a puppy for show only to find out that it is not likely to win.

The perfect dog has yet to be bred. What is looked for is good overall conformation, good shoulders, good hind angulation and a strong back, resulting in a balanced dog with the correct gait. To a certain extent these can be judged in a puppy but this breed can alter so much while growing, as they are not fully mature and at their best until about two years old. Some take even longer. Thus a dog that does a lot of winning as a puppy, can be out of the running as an adult and some unlikely puppies mature into show winners.

The show life of any dog is limited to the time it is at its best, so if you want to carry on showing, you will have to decide if you are going to buy more stock or breed it yourself. If you buy a bitch to show and she does some winning, you can mate her to a top dog and hopefully breed your own winners. A dog will need to get right to the top or establish a good reputation as a sire, before he gets the best bitches.

You will now realize that there is more to showing than just owning a well-bred dog or bitch. Even a suitable one will have to be trained and so will you if you are going to handle the dog

The show stance for a German Shepherd Dog

in the ring. Feeding, exercise and grooming all play a part.

Never try to show a dog which is growing coat as it will look poor beside one in full coat. Extra care should be taken over grooming to make sure that the dog is clean all over and has a shine on its coat. Pay attention to toenails, ears, eyes and tail. Make sure that it is in good hard condition by correct feeding and by giving enough exercise to enable it to muscle up. Soft condition should be a fault in a working breed.

In Britain there are various types of show, from Exemption shows run for charity through Sanction, Limited and Open shows, to the biggest of all, Championship shows. At the last mentioned, the very valued Challenge Certificates are on offer to some or all breeds. These are awarded to the best dog and the best bitch of the breed in question. To become a British champion, a dog must win three of these under different judges at different shows.

In America, show categories run from Matches to Speciality and Points shows, the latter being where one can win points towards a championship status for one's dog. To become an American champion, a dog must win a total of fifteen points and two of these wins must be 'majors' (three or more points

A show stance

won at the same show), won under different judges. The number of points awarded at a show depends on the number of dogs and bitches of the breed actually present and this will vary from area to area.

The definitions of classes at shows are totally different in Britain and America. All would-be exhibitors should obtain the show regulations from their respective Kennel Clubs and study them. However, in neither country can any dog be shown which is not Kennel Club registered. This is one of the reasons why it is so important to make sure that your puppy is registered when you buy it. It could be very disappointing to get the urge to show or breed and find that one's dog, though purebred, was ineligible.

Shows are advertised in the dog magazines. To enter you should write to the show secretary for a schedule and entry form, which must be filled in and returned before the closing date printed on it.

It is up to you to reach the venue on the day of the show at the right time. If it is a championship show, you will have to bench your dog, i.e. tie it into the cubicle which has the dog's ring number on it. Do take a proper leather collar and a benching chain, as dogs can so easily get tangled up if tied on by the slip chain on which they will be exhibited in the ring.

The benching chain

Catalogues will be available, giving details of all the dogs entered and the ring number allotted to your dog. Before you enter the ring, you will be given this number on a card which you will wear when showing. You will most likely be benched near to the ring in which you will be judged but find out all the same because you are responsible for your dog being present for its class when its number is called.

In the ring, once judging starts, you will see the judge, usually taking notes on the dogs as he judges, and at least one steward to get the dogs lined up for the judge, to award the prizes and generally to superintend the organisation inside the ring.

More than any other breed, the German Shepherds need a large ring, as they will be gaited round at a steady trot during the judging and room is needed to see this gait as well as to contain the large number of entries usually there.

When the steward is satisfied that all the entries are present, there will be an initial walk round in numerical order for the judge to have an overall look before each dog is judged individually.

This is where you and the dog will need training, and help should have been forthcoming from your breed club. Not only will the dog have to be in the best condition possible, with its coat in full bloom and carrying the correct amount of weight, it must have learned to stand in the show stance, and to trot on a loose lead to show off its gait. Also the dog will need to have its teeth looked at by the judge.

All this should have been practised daily, so that it seems a natural routine to the dog and will not add to the strangeness of the situation in which it finds itself. Even the regular club nights will not be the same as being in the ring for the first time. You may well be apprehensive yourself and communicate this to the dog.

Teach it to walk into the show stance with its weight evenly on all legs but with one hind leg slightly back, as is the fashion in this breed. Never pull that leg backwards. You will only upset the balance and the dog will quickly move it or have to lean back and spoil its front.

Take your time, watch how others do it and get the advice of an experienced handler. Then, when you can regularly achieve a good stance, teach the dog to stand still in the required position so that the judge can have a good look at it. Make sure that it has been stroked and handled in this position or it may not like a strange judge coming up to do this. By the time the dog is ready to be shown, you should be able to stand it on a loose lead without it moving. Please keep this loose lead when gaiting round. The 'fashion' for showing with a tight lead up under the dog's ears, or 'strung up' as it is called, has nothing

THE SHOW RING

Table

"New" dogs (unseen by Judge)

Handler

Dog being examined by Judge

Judge

"Old" dogs (already seen by Judge in a previous class)

Table

Judge

All dogs

"Once round, please"

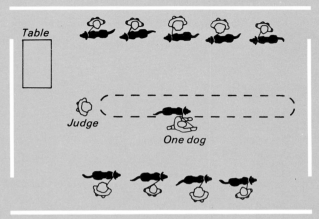

"Once up and down, please"

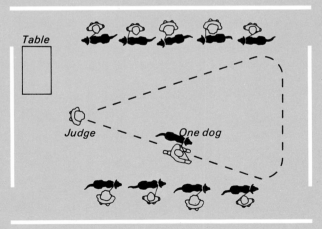

"Triangle, please"

75

to recommend it. It may hide faults in the hands of an expert but it is not to be advised for novice handlers and some judges will not have it. It is very uncomfortable for the dog too.

When your dog's individual examination is over, during which you have shown the dog's teeth and been asked its age, you will be asked to walk it straight up and down and then once round the ring. After that you will have to wait for everyone else to be seen separately and then you will set off all together again in the same order as before. Now the judge will signal, either directly or through the steward, those whom he wishes to move up or go to the front of the line. With a very large class, he will place enough dogs for his requirements and then ask the rest to retire from the ring. Do not be disheartened if you are one of these. The competition is very fierce these days and many good dogs have to go without prizes. Better luck next time.

The remaining dogs in the ring will be placed as the judge decrees, mainly as they move around, until he is satisfied that he has the best dog as the winner and the rest placed according to their merits. Then the steward will call out their numbers and award the rosettes and prize cards with or without prize money as the case may be, as prize money is not always given these days. If your dog does win, keep a careful record of the wins, so that you know exactly which classes it is eligible for at the next show.

Your class over, your dog should be returned to its bench. It is not supposed to be off this except when being shown or taken to relieve itself. There will also be a closing time before which you are not allowed to leave the show.

Professional handlers

If you do not feel able to show off your dog yourself, then you can pay for a professional to handle your dog for you. You will, if you watch many shows, notice that some of the handlers seem to be in every class and these are usually the 'pros'. They are all likely to be in demand, so you will have to book one well before the show at which you are entering. Then see that you are there early enough the first time for the handler to be introduced to the dog. Supply all the necessary details and see that your dog is in the best possible condition and has had some ring training.

In America there are professional handlers who will take the

Showing the teeth for judge's examination

dog for training at home and then take it to shows, but in Britain you are usually expected to have the dog ready and waiting at the show, just to be handled in the class booked and then returned to you, hopefully with a prize.

The judge and judging

The judge is there to award prizes to the dogs that he thinks are the best 'on the day'. Thus, how a dog looks and behaves on that day can affect its placing. All dogs, like people, have their 'off days' when they do not make the most of themselves. At other times they can be in extra fine fettle and show to their best advantage. German Shepherds are sensitive dogs that can easily be put off. Even those used to showing, and those who normally enjoy it, can become bored. Some dogs never like it.

While it is not possible to assess temperament accurately in the show ring, the judge should discard any obviously shy or aggressive dogs. A dog with the correct temperament for the breed should not be difficult to train to move and be handled on a loose lead. The judge should be able to tell if the dog is unduly worried by the look in its eye and the way it uses its ears.

The judge has the right to withhold the prizes if he thinks that the dogs present are not up to the Breed Standard. It is his task to find dogs that are as near to the Standard as possible and then to decide his winners by summing up each dog as a whole. All judges have their pet likes and dislikes but these should not influence them when judging.

Breeding

As with most other breeds, the German Shepherd bitch comes into season twice a year, usually in the early spring and late summer. A bitch usually has her first season at around ten months old and then every six months after that. Her first season can be earlier than this, so she should be watched from about nine months for the first signs. Each bitch will tend to have her own fixed cycle of just over or under six months.

This breed develops slowly and bitches are not ready to have a litter until they are nearly two years old. Their third season should be aimed for, as on average this will occur at about twenty-two months, so that when the bitch whelps nine weeks later she will be just about two years old. The only thing is that spring puppies are to be preferred to autumn ones, so a well grown bitch of eighteen months might have her litter then rather than in the autumn. It is not advisable to breed a first litter later than three years old. A bitch should only have one litter a year up to about the age of eight. There should not be more than two years between litters.

Well before the bitch is due to come into season, a suitable dog should have been selected and a service booked for the probable date. Then on the day that she starts her season the owner of the stud dog should be notified of the likely day for the mating.

The bitch should be in the finest possible condition and have been wormed.

She will normally be ready for mating about fourteen days after her season started when the coloured discharge has lessened. Bitches vary when they are ready but from the tenth to the eighteenth day is a rough guide. When ready the bitch will raise her tail and move it to one side when stroked over her hindquarters.

A bitch brought up in the company of dogs is usually easy to get mated but if she has been kept as an only one, she should be introduced to the dog beforehand. Also for a first mating she should be taken by her owner. She should have had sufficient exercise to relieve herself beforehand and for a young bitch an experienced stud dog should be chosen which will not frighten her unnecessarily. The management of the stud dog must be left to his owner or handler and the bitch held on a lead to prevent any injury to the dog.

When the dog has mounted the bitch and effected a tie, this can last for a few minutes or over half an hour. Afterwards the bitch should be kept quiet for a time before the return journey home.

Make sure that she does not have the chance to get mated by other dogs until her season is finished, that is for another ten days at least.

After mating no change in routine is necessary for the bitch for the first few weeks. Do not start to give her extra food or you may end up with a bitch which you think is in whelp but is in fact only too fat. Nine weeks or sixty-three days is the average time from mating to whelping, but German Shepherd bitches seem to like to whelp two or three days earlier than that.

Whelping box with a canvas front

From half way (four and a half weeks) food can be slightly increased. If she is carrying a litter it should show by the fifth week and then her food should be divided into two or three meals a day. Keep off fattening foods but increase the meat and supplements and add a milky meal with an egg occasionally. Do not overfeed, and keep up regular exercise.

The bitch will whelp more easily if she is slim, although this is a breed which normally whelps without trouble.

The bitch should be introduced to her whelping quarters well before the time due or she will not settle there. She must have a box that allows her to lie out at full stretch but with a rail round it that will prevent her from lying on the pups. Some bitches are more prone to do this than others. When she is due to whelp, the bitch will usually go off her food and then a few hours later become uneasy and restless. She should not be left alone and a veterinary surgeon should be notified of the impending arrival.

Normally the puppies will arrive at regular intervals without any help and the bitch will instinctively set about cleaning them up, etc., but any prolonged straining of more than two hours without the arrival of a puppy should be treated with caution and professional advice sought. Watch the bitch carefully for the first forty-eight hours after whelping in case she has retained any afterbirth that might cause infection.

It is as well to have her looked over by a veterinary surgeon even after a simple whelping if you are not sure. Otherwise do not allow anyone, person or dog, to come near the whelping quarters to upset the bitch.

For a first litter, or with a restless bitch, it is advisable to put each puppy as it is born into a smaller box near her, so that she can get on with the next arrival. However, some bitches will not like you doing this.

Most bitches like a drink of milk during whelping and water should be available.

When you are satisfied that the whelping is finished, remove any soiled bedding, gently clean up the bitch and see that she is comfortable before leaving the pups happily sucking. She should not be left with too many to rear. Eight should be enough for any bitch and preferably fewer for a first litter.

In a large litter there may be weaklings which will not survive the first few days.

The bitch should be kept on a light diet for two days after

whelping, with plenty to drink. From then on she is going to need a great deal to eat if she is to cope with the requirements of her hungry family.

For about the first three weeks, except for the removal of the hind dewclaws (if any) by an experienced breeder or veterinary surgeon at about five days old, the pups are not going to need much attention and you can enjoy watching them feed and grow.

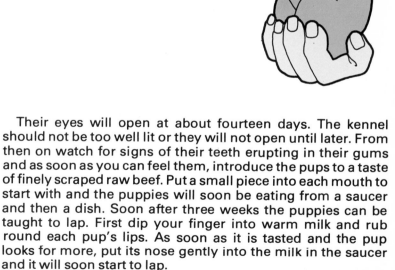

The correct way to hold a puppy

Their eyes will open at about fourteen days. The kennel should not be too well lit or they will not open until later. From then on watch for signs of their teeth erupting in their gums and as soon as you can feel them, introduce the pups to a taste of finely scraped raw beef. Put a small piece into each mouth to start with and the puppies will soon be eating from a saucer and then a dish. Soon after three weeks the puppies can be taught to lap. First dip your finger into warm milk and rub round each pup's lips. As soon as it is tasted and the pup looks for more, put its nose gently into the milk in the saucer and it will soon start to lap.

Now you will have to start a weaning programme of up to six feeds a day, gradually keeping the bitch away longer and

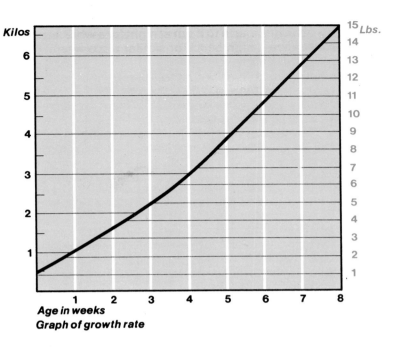

Kilos / *Lbs.*

Age in weeks
Graph of growth rate

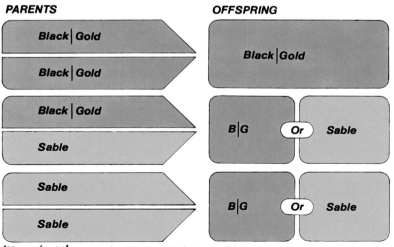

PARENTS	OFFSPRING
Black	Gold Black	Gold	Black	Gold
Black	Gold Sable	B	G **Or** Sable
Sable Sable	B|G **Or** Sable

(Note – 'gold' means the range of lighter markings from tan to cream)
Simple Colour Inheritance Chart

83

longer during the day. She will usually be fed up with the pups anyway, so just let her return to them at night for a while. In any case, she must have a high bench or similar place where she can rest away from them.

Remember to start their house training by putting them in the same place each time that they are woken up.

By six weeks the bitch will probably want to leave them altogether, except for an occasional visit to help dry off her milk. This, by now, is of very little food value to the puppies and she will dry off quickly if they are only allowed to suck for a short while.

By this age the puppies should be having two meat meals and two milky ones to which suitable cereal has been gradually introduced in the form of baby cereals and puppy meal.

A last night drink of milk will settle them down when the bitch is first taken away. Now they should be on the diet sheet that will be provided when they go to their new owners from eight weeks onwards. They must be wormed as early as possible on veterinary advice.

If you bought your bitch as a companion, then think carefully before breeding from her. It is not necessary for her health that she is bred from and, in such a numerically large breed, there are already more than enough puppies available. In fact, unless you are an established breeder, you may find difficulty in selling the puppies to suitable homes.

It is sometimes possible to obtain a bitch on breeding terms. For example, instead of paying the full price for the bitch, puppies from her next litter are returned to the previous owner. Terms vary; sometimes the bitch returns as well after the litter and sometimes she stays permanently with the new owner. Whatever is agreed must be clearly stated in writing at the time, to avoid disputes later.

Choosing a stud dog

It is not enough to like a dog, as he may not suit your bitch's bloodlines. Mating a champion dog to a champion bitch will not necessarily produce more champions, so using a dog just because he is a champion is not sufficient.

A study of pedigrees is necessary if you wish to improve your stock or keep up to the Standard.

If you have a particular fault in the bitch that you wish to

correct, see that the dog you choose does not have this fault too or you will tend to fix it in the offspring. Equally, see that you do not overcompensate. The dog should be correct for the failing that you wish to improve. For example, don't mate a bitch without sufficient hind angulation to a dog with too much, for it will not even out. Use a dog with the correct angulation and which is known to pass this on to his offspring.

If the stock sired, to a variety of bitches, by any dog that you like is mainly of the type you want to breed, see if any of these bitches are related to yours. If so, you may have found the dog you are looking for, to suit your bitch.

Approach the owner of the stud dog chosen to make sure that your bitch will be accepted and, if so, book the probable date well ahead.

The stud dog should be kept in good hard condition and have the correct temperament for this breed.

Make sure that you know the stud fee to be charged. Most breeders will supply you with a stud card giving details of fee and pedigree and also any conditions attached. The stud fee is payable as soon as the mating is effected, only one mating being the usual procedure for this breed. Most stud dog owners will, however, give a free repeat mating at her next season to a bitch that fails to have a litter, but these conditions must be agreed at the time of mating. It is usual to ask for a veterinary certificate to say that the bitch has missed. Any other conditions, such as a puppy in lieu of stud fee, should be clearly stated in writing to avoid misunderstanding later.

The owner of a dog bought and kept as a companion will be well advised not to use him at stud on the one or two bitches that he is likely to get. Once used, the dog is sure to become unsettled when there are any bitches in season in the neighbourhood.

Health Index

A dog exhibiting any of the following symptoms should be taken to a qualified veterinary surgeon for a diagnosis and the correct treatment.

Loss of appetite It is not natural for dogs to go off their food. They are usually greedy eaters, although they may be spoilt by too much 'fussing' as puppies. Temporary loss of appetite usually happens when puppies are removed from the competition of their litter mates and have so much else to interest them in their new surroundings. They will eat when hungry if given time to settle.

There is a tendency to overfeed adult dogs, which need less food than while growing. At any time any food not eaten up straight away should be removed. It never hurts a dog to miss one meal but the time to worry is when a good eater suddenly goes off its food.

Loss of condition If a dog is eating well and is not taking more exercise than usual but persists in losing weight, then something is wrong. It may be worms, but it may be more serious.

Diarrhoea Loose bowel actions once in a while are not unusual as the diet may have been varied but this condition must not be allowed to continue without finding out the cause. With a puppy there should be a return to normal motions at the usual times within twenty-four hours, and even with an adult loose and frequent bowel actions should be taken seriously if they persist into a second day. If sickness is present as well, then advice should be sought at once.

Constipation The passing of small, hard motions, except after a session of eating bones (and you must consult your veterinary surgeon about giving your dog bones anyway), should not be allowed to continue, especially if accompanied by straining. It may be that there is not enough roughage in the diet, which can be supplied by sprinkling bran on the food, but laxatives should be given only under veterinary supervision and the cause of the constipation looked into.

Scratching No dog should need to scratch or nibble at itself. Look for fleas or lice and if present use a recommended insecticide or if necessary bath the dog. Make sure that all bedding is renewed. Any dog can pick up fleas from time to time and do not delay in getting rid of them.

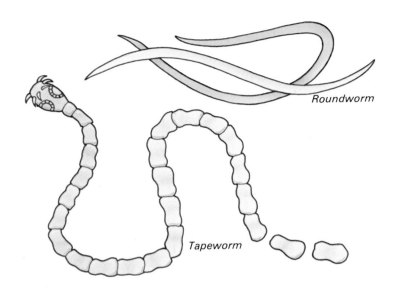
Roundworm

Tapeworm

Adult flea

Biting louse

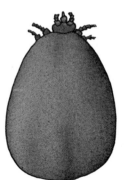
Engorged female tick

Mite (microscopic)

Sucking louse

Parasites

Skin troubles German Shepherd Dogs are not unduly prone to skin troubles, so any bare or sore patches that appear should be carefully examined. The trouble may be internal.

Ears Scratching at the ears or shaking the head is a sign that all is not well inside the ear. Apart from cleaning out gently, do not poke about. The ear is very sensitive and needs to be treated with care. Consult your veterinary surgeon.

Worms Most dogs suffer from worms of one sort or another from time to time. Even when properly wormed as puppies, they become re-infected and it is as well to check up as your veterinary surgeon advises. Worm at once if any are seen in the motions. A harsh coat on a dog is usually a sign of worms.

Fits A fit can result from a variety of causes but it must be taken seriously and the reason or reasons determined. Epileptic fits occur in dogs and have been found to be hereditary, although of a complicated inheritance pattern. These can be diagnosed and satisfactory treatment provided in some cases.

Eyes Eyes can become sore and inflamed from draughts, etc., and may need cleaning with an eye wash. Runny eyes should be diagnosed at once.

Inoculations All puppies should be inoculated against hard-pad, distemper, hepatitis and leprospiral diseases at the earliest recommended time. They will then need 'boosters' to maintain their resistance to these diseases. You will be given a certificate stating the date when the puppy was first inoculated and this will also tell you when the boosters are due. Most boarding kennels will require an up-to-date certificate before accepting a dog in to board.

Hip dysplasia (HD) Varying degrees of this condition are found in most breeds of dog. The hip joint is a cup-shaped cavity, the acetabulum, into which fits the rounded head of the femur. Ligaments help to hold the head in position and further support is given by muscles surrounding the joint.

Any deviation from the normal can result in lameness or painful movement. Lameness, however, can result from other causes and hip dysplasia can be confirmed only by X-ray under a general anaesthetic. It is not possible to look at a dog's movement and state that it has hip dysplasia without confirmation by X-ray.

The condition is hereditary but of complicated inheritance and even breeding from parents with 'good hips' can and does result in puppies with dysplasia. At the same time poor or

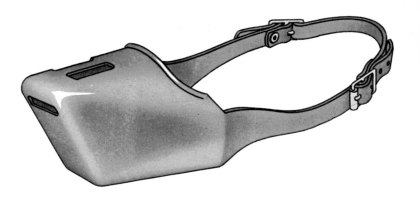

Plastic muzzle for possible use as an anti-rabies measure

over-feeding and too much exercising of the young puppy can affect the final condition of the hips.

The X-raying of stock to be used for breeding or working is a necessary precaution but should not be necessary for the companion dog unless it is lame or in pain. Many dogs which have lived happy, healthy lives, would, if X-rayed, have shown a degree of HD.

LIST OF USEFUL ADDRESSES

The Kennel Club, 1 Clarges Street, Piccadilly, London W1Y 8AB, England, for registration and transfer forms, etc. Publishes *The Kennel Club Year Book* annually, and *The Kennel Gazette* monthly.

The American Kennel Club, 51 Madison Avenue, New York, N.Y. 10010, USA.

The Alsatian League and Club of Great Britain, Whitmore Vale End, Hindhead, Surrey, England. Members receive third party insurance cover and reduced entry fees to the Open and Championship shows held each year. Publishes *The League Magazine* five times a year, and *The League Handbook* bi-annually. These and other mail order items are available from this address.

The British Alsatian Association (BAA), 55a South Road, Erdington, Birmingham 23, England. Has branches throughout the country catering for Obedience and Working Trials. Members receive third party insurance cover and reduced entry fees to these and the Open and Championship shows held each year. The Association is a member of the World Union of G.S.D. Clubs. Publishes *The Shepherd Dog Magazine* four times a year.

The Associated Sheep, Police and Army Dog Society (ASPADS), Barefields, Dunton Road, Laindon, Essex, England. Holds Working Trials and an Open Breed Show each year.

The Central Dog Registry Limited, 49 Marloes Road, London W8 6LA, England, for tattooing.

Verein für Deutsche Schäferhunde (SV) Hauptgeschaftsstelle, 89 Augsberg 17, Beim Schnarrbrunnen 4-6, Ende Predigigerberg, W. Germany. Publishes, in English, *The German Shepherd in Word and Picture* by von Stephanitz.

The German Shepherd Dog Club of America Inc. Membership Chairman: Mrs. Helen Fisher, 8139 38th Street N., Lake Elmo, MN 55042, USA. Publishes monthly *The German Shepherd Dog Review,* editor Mrs. P.L. Bennet, PO Box 1221, Lancaster, Pa 17604, USA.

DOG MAGAZINES

Pure Bred Dogs, the American Kennel Gazette, published by the American Kennel Club.
Dog World, 22 New Street, Ashford, Kent, England.
Our Dogs, 5 Oxford Road Station Approach, Manchester 1, England.

READING LIST

Delinger, M., Paramoure, A. and Umlauff, G. (revised J. Bennett), *The Complete German Shepherd Dog.* Howell Book House, 1972.
Elliott, P. and N. *The Complete Alsatian.* Kaye and W., 1975.
Goldbecker, Capt. W. and Hart, E. *This is the German Shepherd.* T.F.H. Publications.
Pickup, Madeleine. *The Alsatian Owner's Encyclopaedia.* Pelham Books, 1974.
Schwabacher, J. and Gray, T. *The Alsatian.* Popular Dogs Publications.
Willis, M.B. *The German Shepherd Dog, History, Development and Genetics.*

Index

Distributors for
Bartholomew Pet Books

Australia
Book Trade: Tudor Distributors Pty. Limited, 14 Mars Road,
Lane Cove 2066, New South Wales, Australia

Canada
Pet Trade: Burgham Sales Ltd., 558 McNicoll Avenue,
Willowdale (Toronto), Ontario, Canada M2H 2E1
Book Trade: Clarke Irwin and Company, Limited,
791 St. Clair Avenue W., Toronto, Canada M6C 1B

New Zealand
Pet Trade: Masterpet Products Limited,
7 Kaiwharawhara Road, Wellington, New Zealand
Book Trade: Whitcoulls Limited, Trade Department, Private Ba
Auckland, Wellington, or Christchurch, New
Zealand

South Africa
Book Trade: McGraw-Hill Book Company (S.A.) (Pty.) Limited,
P.O. Box 23423, Joubert Park, Johannesburg,
South Africa

U.S.A.
Pet Trade: Pet Supply Imports Inc., P.O. Box 497, Chicago,
Illinois, U.S.A.
Book Trade: The Two Continents Publishing Group Limited,
30 East 42nd Street, New York, N.Y. 10017, U.S.A.